T0058976

SCHIRMER'S LIBRARY OF MUSICAL CLASSICS

Vol. 624

LUDWIG VAN BEETHOVEN

Op. 58

Concerto No. IV

For the Piano

Provided with Fingering, and with a
Complete Arrangement, for Piano,
of the Orchestral Accompaniment

by

FRANZ KULLAK

The Introduction and Notes
translated from the German
by

DR. THEODORE BAKER

Concerto No. I, Op. 15, In C major — Library Vol. 621

Concerto No. II, Op. 19, in B flat major — Library Vol. 622

Concerto No. III, Op. 37, in C minor — Library Vol. 623

→ Concerto No. IV, Op. 58, in G major, Library Vol. 624

Concerto No. V, Op. 73, in E flat major — Library Vol. 625

ISBN 978-0-7935-5192-7

G. SCHIRMER, Inc.

DISTRIBUTED BY

Copyright © 1901, 1929 (Renewed) by G. Schirmer, Inc. (ASCAP) New York, NY
International Copyright Secured. All Rights Reserved.
Warning: Unauthorized reproduction of this publication is
prohibited by Federal law and subject to criminal prosecution.

Fourth Concerto.

Dedicated to his Imperial Highness Archduke Rudolph of Austria.*

Finished 1806 (?). Published in August, 1808, by the Kunst– und Industrie-Comptoir, Vienna and Pesth. Performed for the first time in public (1) by the composer on Dec. 22, 1808, in the Theater an der Wien.

Allegro moderato. (M.M., following Czerny (2), ♩ = 116.)

L. van BEETHOVEN, Op.58.
New revised.edition, 1883.

* In the original edition in oblong form, the complete title, surrounded by a wreath, reads: *"Viertes Concert für das Pianoforte mit 2 Violinen, Viola, Flöte, 2 Hautbois, 2 Clarinetten, 2 Hörnern, 2 Fagotten, Trompetten* [sic], *Pauken, Violoncell und Bass. Seiner Kaiserlichen Hoheit, dem Erzherzog Rudolph von Oesterreich unterthänigst gewidmet von L. van Beethoven. Op. 58.* [Outside the wreath, to the left]: *592.* [Below]: *Wien und Pesth im Verlage des Kunst und Industrie Comptoirs."* [No price given.]

(1) According to Thayer (Life of Beethoven, vol. III. pp. 6-8), this concerto was played as early as March, 1807 in the salons of Prince L(obkowitz).
(2) Carl Czerny, "Die Kunst des Vortrags", Supplement to the great Pianoforte-Method op. 500.
(3) 1 Flute, 2 Oboes, 2 Clarinets, 2 Horns, 2 Bassoons, and Strings (Q.)— Trumpets and Drums not till last movement.

Printed in the U.S.A.

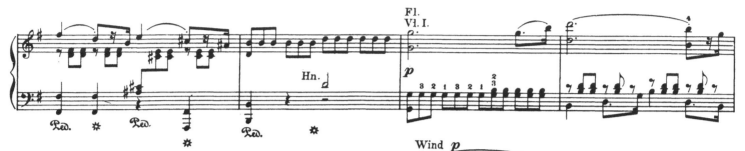

3

4

(1) All appoggiaturas in this Concerto, with the sole exception of that beginning the trill $\widehat{tr}$ on p. 67, are *crossed* in the original edition; whereas the original impression of the C-minor Concerto, which was published by the same firm 4 years previously, contains only uncrossed appoggiaturas.

(2) The f added to this chord in recent editions (likewise a preceding *cresc.*) is not given in the original impression.

(3) To facilitate the study (or memorizing) of the shorter Tutti for the soloist, they are given in his part in a simplified form.

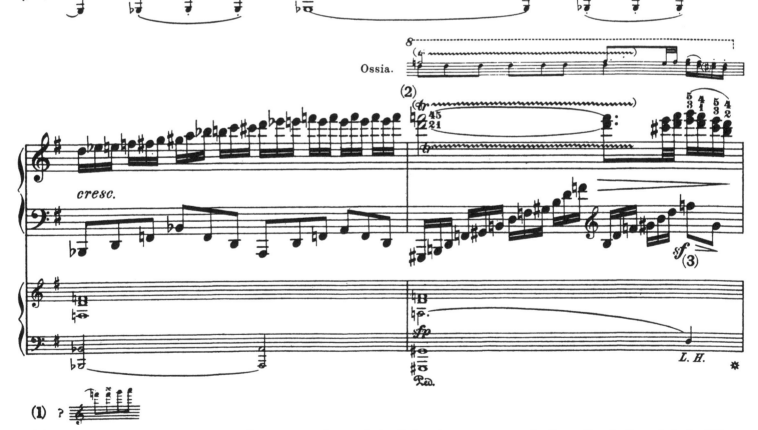

(1)

(2) It is evident that the trill-signs (in parenthesis) and the light slurs were merely forgotten in the original edition.

(3) Compare Note on p. 20.

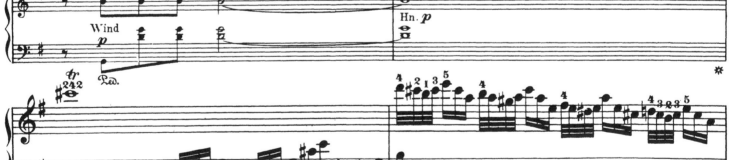

(1) Often, in later editions, *fp*.
(2) Here also frequently *fp*.

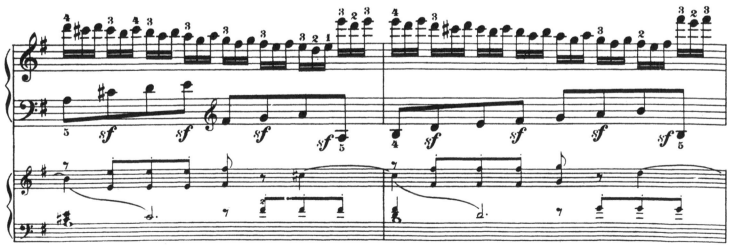

(1) In some editions this *f* reads *ff*, in correspondence with the parallel passage found on p. 30, which, how-ever, is more heavily orchestrated.

(2) *p*, in correspondence with the parallel passage in some editions, is omitted in the original edition. Also see Note on p. 30.

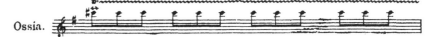

(1) The reading in the original edition, ![engraver's error notation], which is reproduced in some later ones, we consider to be an engraver's error.

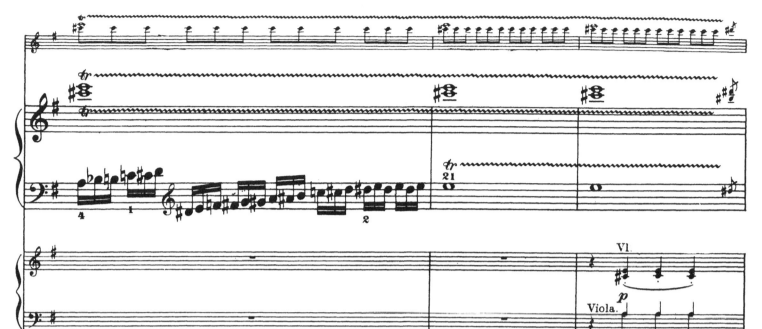

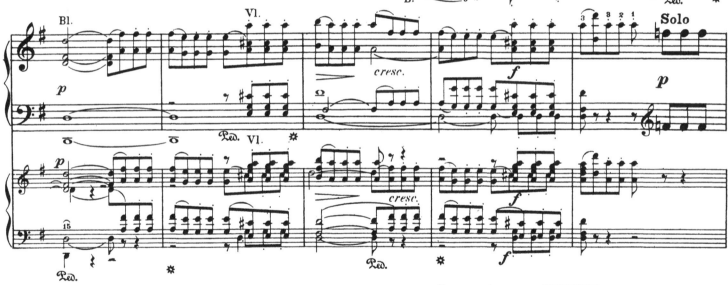

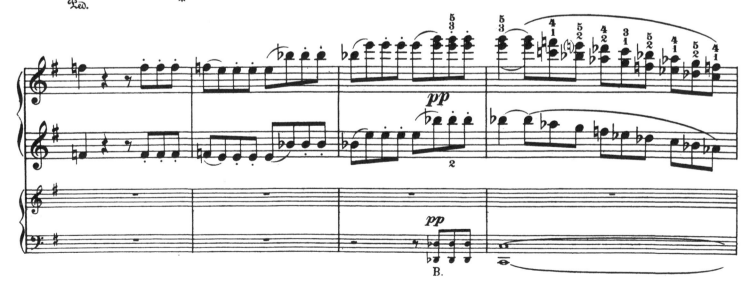

(1) Breitkopf & Härtel, and Peters, repeat the "Ped." 6 times every other measure. —Czerny says, furthermore (Thayer, II, 348): "He [Beethoven] employed the pedal very often, much more than is indicated in his works".

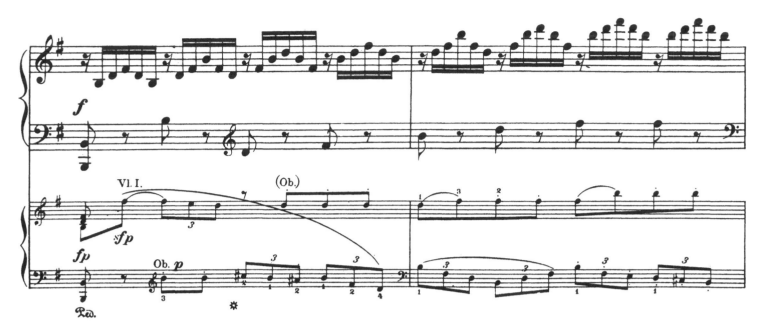

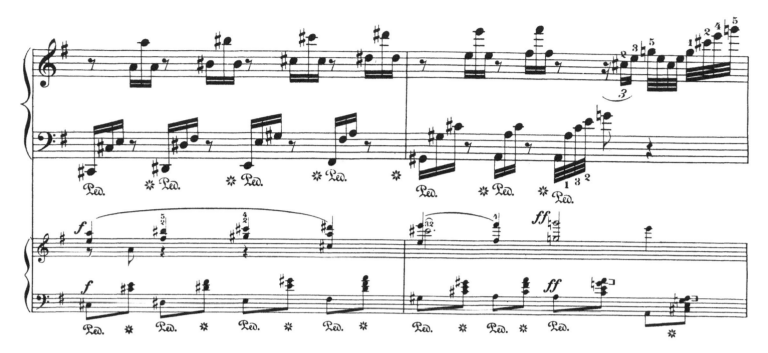

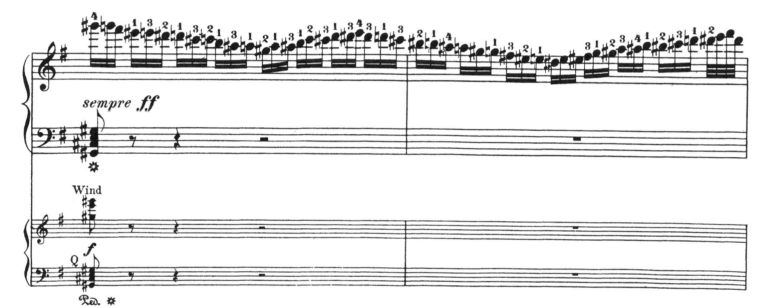

(1) Properly ⎯⎯. Most accents of this kind were given in this form, particularly in the last movement; while, on the other hand, an accent-sign probably meaning a simple diminuendo occurred on p. 6:

On this head we remark:

(a) Differing from our present usage, both the expression-marks and all notes for the left hand, in the Tutti, are as large as those in the Soli.

(b) In the arrangement of the Tutti, the bass part is but very seldom doubled in the lower octave (double-bass part).

(c) The ff in the third measure is not given at all in the score at this point, but does occur instead of the f in the first of these three measures.

(d) Although the entrance of the solo part is sufficiently indicated (at least for the right hand) by the word "Solo", Czerny nevertheless writes (in his "Kunst des Vortrags") the whole of this third measure in large notes:

"The theme  in the first two measures with the greatest possible energy".

(It looks as if Czerny had written from memory; in the notation, at least, he does not follow the printed text [𝄢 instead of 𝄢].) We shall not decide, whether Beethoven played this last measure, at the public performance with orchestra, in the complete form indicated by Czerny. Also compare a similar passage in the last movement, p. 60.

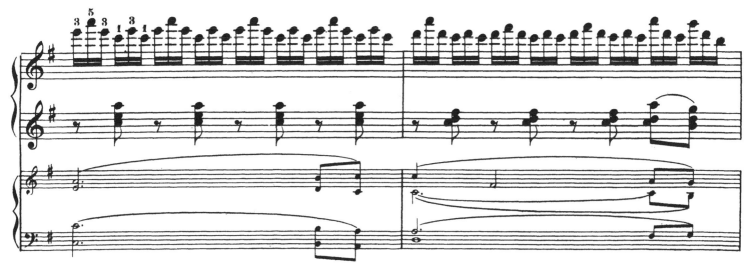

(1) Br. & H., also Peters, give "*p* 𝆏𝆐."; omitted in the original.

(1) Given wrongly ∾ in the original edition.

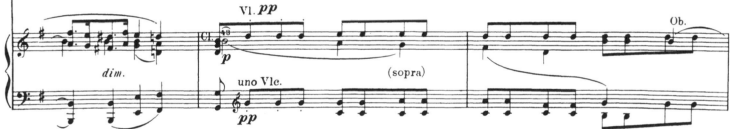

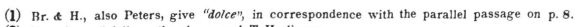

(1) Br. & H., also Peters, give *"dolce"*, in correspondence with the parallel passage on p. 8.
(2) This *"cresc."* follows the above, and T. Haslinger.

(1) Variant after Breitkopf & Härtel, like the parallel passage on p. 9. employing d^4:

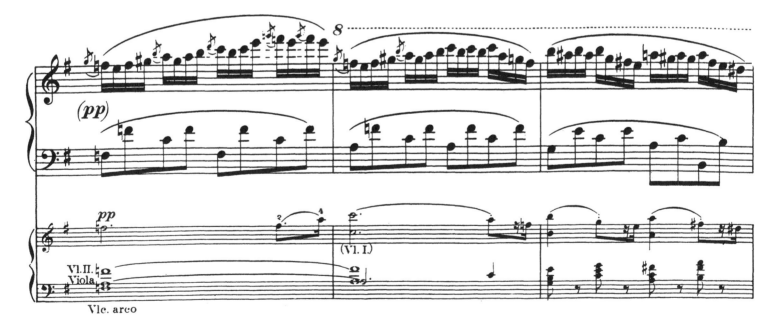

(1) This *p* follows recent editions, like the parallel passage on p. 9; then *pp*.

Variant in recent editions:

(1) Br. & H. give  (not in the score), like the parallel passage on p.10.

(1) Though reluctant to deviate from Beethoven's original readings, we find this variant of recent editions the more deserving of consideration from the fact, that by the omission of the note *d¹*, then not at the composer's command, the point of the original thought (*cf.* the parallel passage on p. 11) is, so to speak, broken off. On the other hand, this fact appears to throw special light on the repeated ***p*** (not found in the parallel passage); for here, according to the original reading, the highest tone *g³*, in *forte,* would be apt to drown the melody-tone *d* of the flute, whereas in the parallel passage the *a* of the oboe, besides its greater natural intensity, is essentially reinforced by the closing chord of the pianoforte.— We advance no opinion as to whether the repeated ***p*** might have been merely forgotten, in the parallel passage.

(1) Acc. to the parallel passage,

(1) In Br. & H., and P., likewise with ⌢.
(2) 2 Cadenzas by Beethoven; see Appendix.

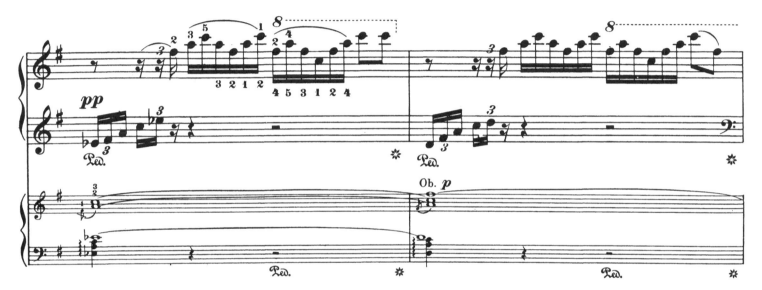

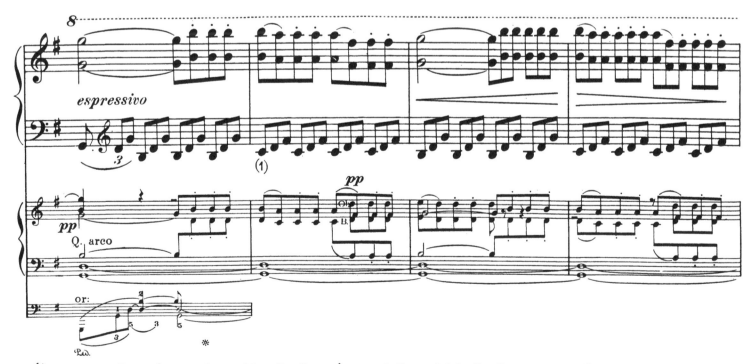

(1) Compare Czerny's remark touching Beethoven's use of the pedal in the Largo of the C-minor Concerto (p.23 of our edition). Without abating our reverence for the immortal master, we cannot avoid recognition of the rules for the modern employment of the pedal, requiring a more frequent change or interruption of its effect.

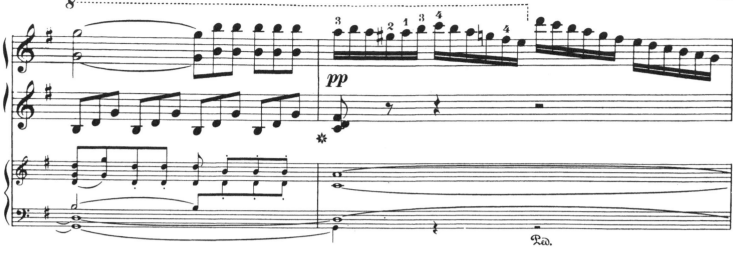

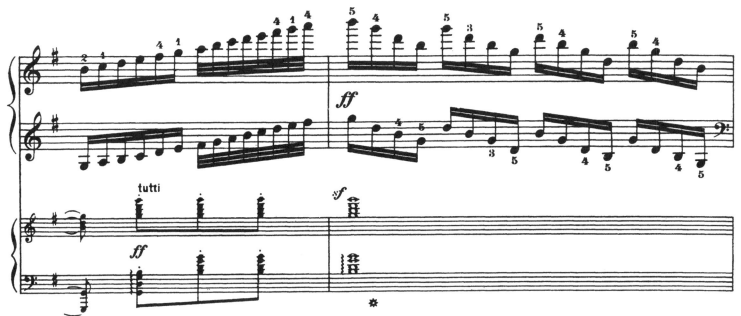

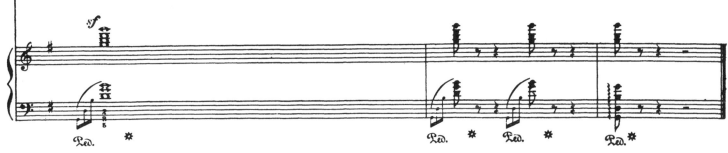

Andante con moto. ♪= 100. (Czerny: ♩ = 84.)

Dans tout cet Andante on tient levée la Pédale, qui ne fait sonner qu'une corde.
Au signe 𝕻𝖉. on lève outre cela les étouffoirs. (1)

(1) "Throughout this *Andante* keep the pedal lifted which allows only one string to sound. At the sign 𝕻𝖉., likewise lift the dampers". [This means: Hold down the soft pedal throughout this *Andante*; take the loud pedal at the
sign 𝕻𝖉.]

(2) Czerny sets a "*pp*" before this "*molto cantabile*"; these two directions appear hardly congruous, especially as
the soft pedal was already required.

(3) Recent editions, which indicate the Tutti only as interpolations in the Solo part, give "*pp*" here and in the 6
following solo entrances. The original edition, which carries on the orchestral accompaniment uninterruptedly from
this point to the close on two staves above the solo part, fills out the hiatuses in the latter with rests, and provides
no new expression-mark for the successive later solo entrances.

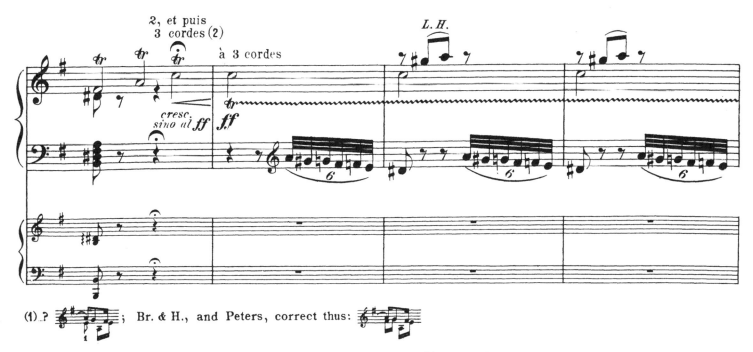

(1) ? ; Br. & H., and Peters, correct thus:

(2) An effect practicable only on a trichord pianoforte with *shifting*-pedal.

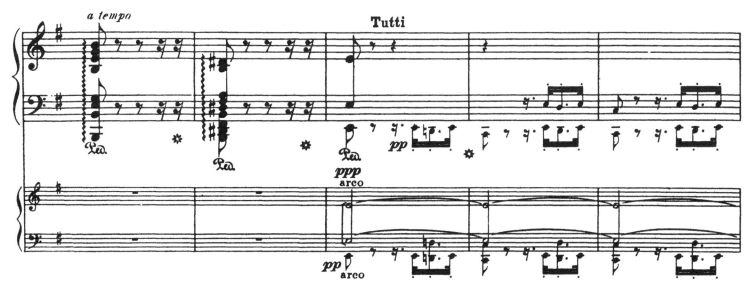

Segue il Rondo.

(1) It is probably a mere mistake that the original edition gives a bar here (end of the page). Br. & H. give a ⌢ over the last *tr*; Peters ditto.

(2) In the original edition, probably mistake:

41

Rondo.
Vivace. ♩= 132. (Czerny: ♩= 138.)

(1) Czerny adds *mf*.

(1) Br. & H., likewise Peters (the latter, however, not in the score), correct, in correspondence with the parallel passage on p.55, etc. Here the original edition gives only f♯.

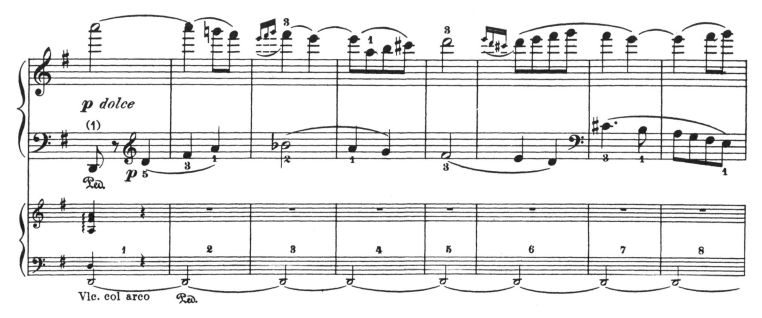

(1) Br. & H.'s score adds an *f* at the first eighth-note in the bass.
(2) We add this *f*, following Br. & H. and Peters, in correspondence with the parallel passage on p. 55, also taking into consideration the *f* in the Violoncello and Violin I.

(1) In the parallel passage, p. 56, only *f*.

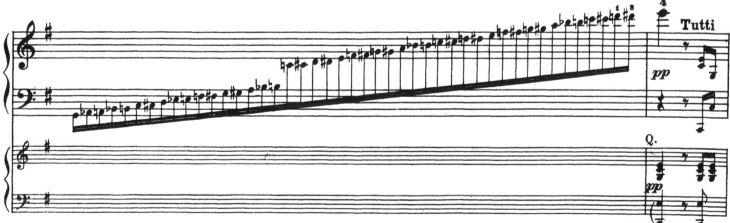

(1) ⌐‾‾¬ and the figures were added by the editor to facilitate reading.

(2) In B. & H., and Peters, the direction *"ad libitum"* is added to this Cadenza.

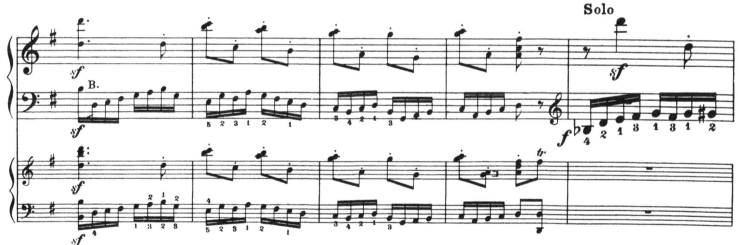

56 Tutti

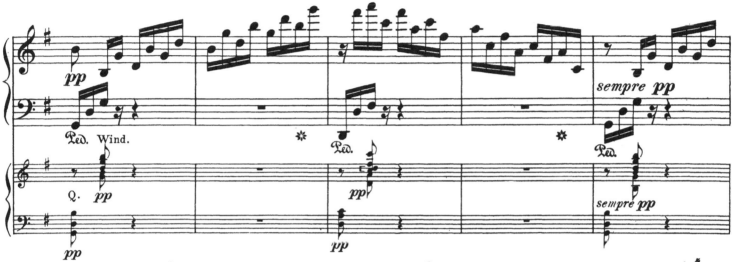

(1) *cresc.*, acc. to the analogous passage on p.47. B. & H. also give ⤙

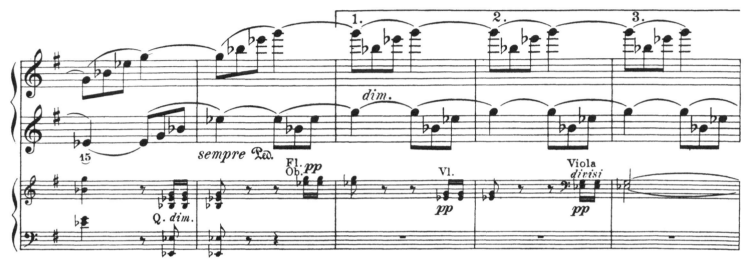

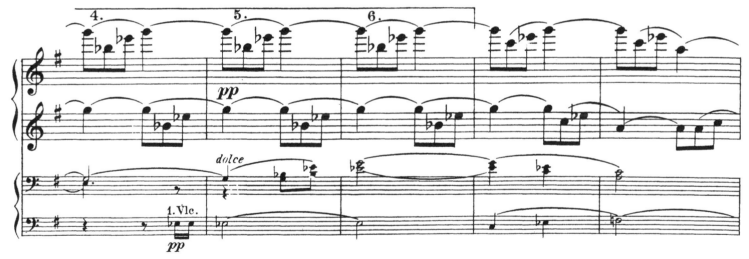

(1) Acc. to the Orig. Edition: etc. See Note on p.22.

(2) Here, too, the original edition gives *ad lib.*

(1) "Let the Cadenza be short." — For Cadenza by Beethoven, see Appendix.

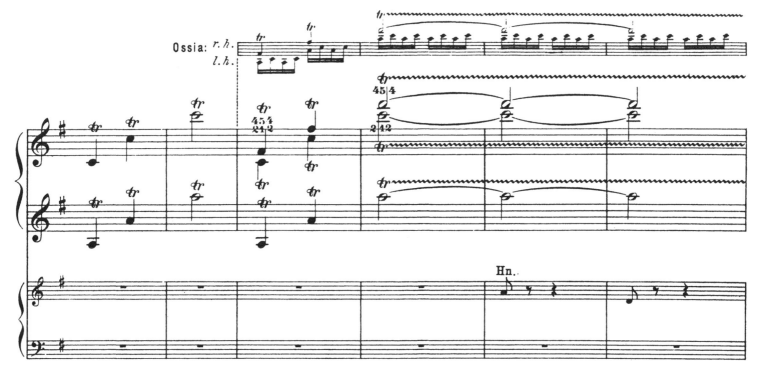

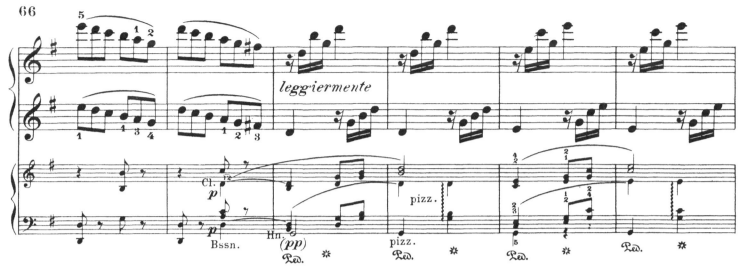

(1) Fingering by Czerny.

(1) "and in the closing measures, *accelerando*" (?). — For the rest, this direction would be in keeping with an observation by Ferdinand Ries concerning the piano-playing of his teacher, Beethoven: ".... In general he himself played his compositions very capriciously, but usually kept strict time, only occasionally (though seldom) somewhat pressing the tempo" (Thayer, II, 346.)

Touching the "capriciousness" of his playing, Czerny says: "Astonishing as was his extempore playing, he was often less happy in the performance of his engraved compositions; for, never having time or patience to restudy anything, his success depended chiefly on chance and caprice." (Thayer, II, 348.)

(1) The unrhythmical (as well as indistinct) slurring of the original edition (1, 2, 2, 3 or 3, 2, 3 measures) seemed to us unnecessary of imitation. Both Br. & H. and Peters also slur groups of four measures.

Appendix.
Cadenzas.(1)
No. 1.
To the First Movement.
„Cadenza (ma senza cadere)." (2)

(1) In Nottebohm's Thematic Catalogue of Beethoven's compositions, these Cadenzas are enumerated among the authentic ones; the autographs, according to the same authority, are in the possession of Breitkopf & Härtel. Not published during the composer's lifetime, they were first printed, to the best of our knowledge, by the above firm.

(2) Acc. to Nottebohm, this title was written by Beethoven himself. Also *cf.* Thayer's Chronological Catalogue, No 131.

(3) Br. & H. give *f* instead of *d,* probably by mistake (once). The Fischhof copy, in the Berlin Royal Library, reads like our edition.

Poco sostenuto.

Tempo moderato. **Presto.**

(1) According to the above-mentioned copy, "*p*". (?)

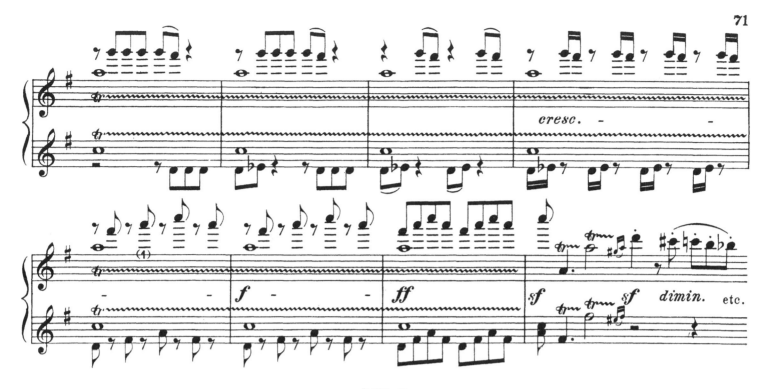

cresc. - - -

- f - - ff - sf dimin. etc.

№ 2.
To the First Movement.

Allegro.

(1) Acc. to Czerny (Pianoforte - Method, Part I), the auxiliary note of the trill coincident with the melody-note may be omitted.

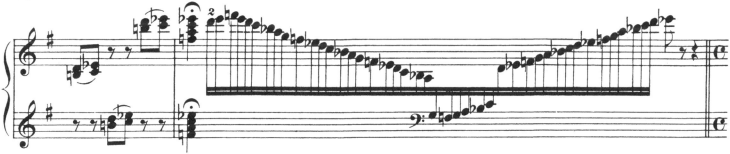

Tempo I.

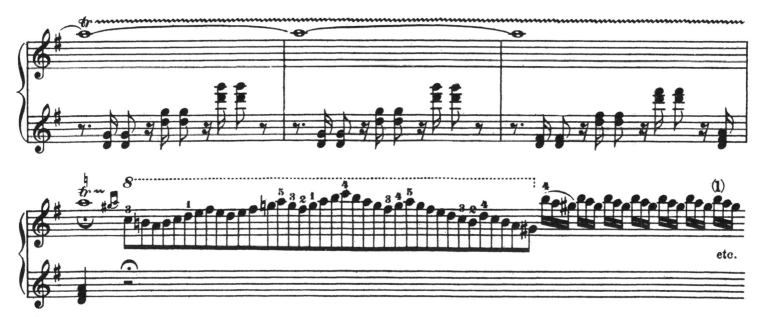

etc.

(1) Another copy, in a different hand from the one in Prof. Fischhof's literary remains (R. Library, Berlin), repeats the last three notes once more.

Nº 3.
To the Rondo.

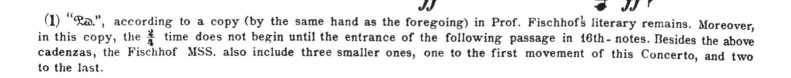

(1) "Ped.", according to a copy (by the same hand as the foregoing) in Prof. Fischhof's literary remains. Moreover, in this copy, the $\frac{2}{4}$ time does not begin until the entrance of the following passage in 16th- notes. Besides the above cadenzas, the Fischhof MSS. also include three smaller ones, one to the first movement of this Concerto, and two to the last.